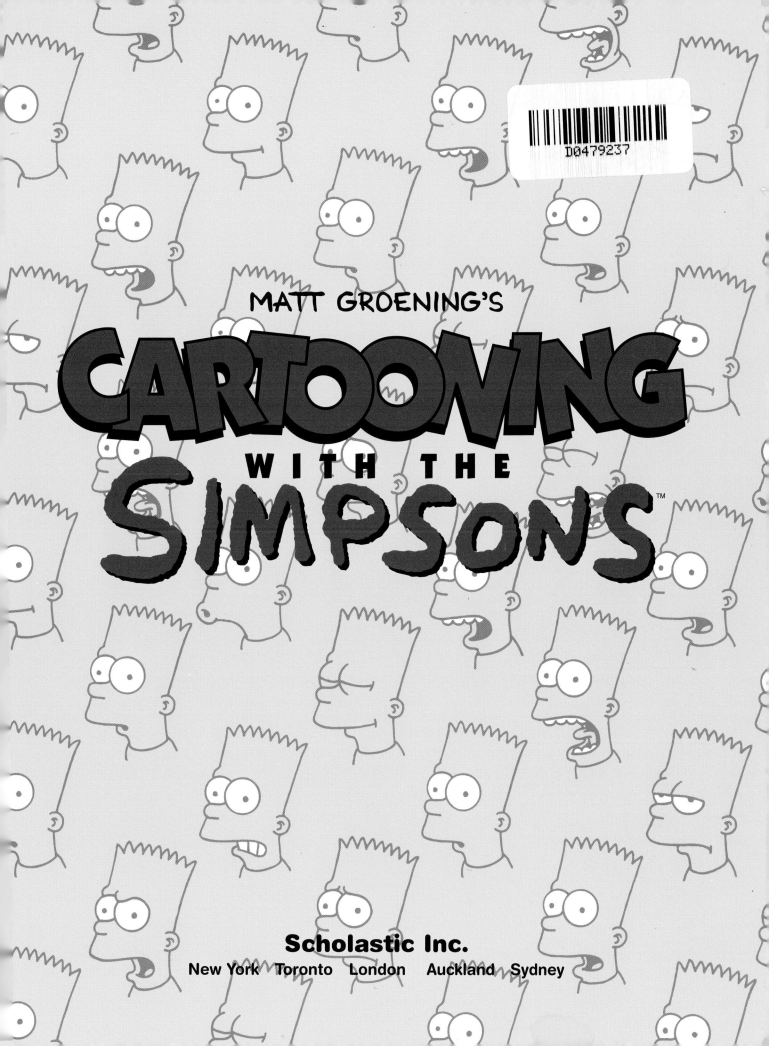

MATT GROENING'S

CARTOONING

WITH THE

SIMPSONS™

Scholastic Inc.
New York Toronto London Auckland Sydney

Dedicated to the memory of Snowball I:

You may be gone, but we still
remember how to draw you.

The Simpsons™, created by Matt Groening, are the copyrighted and trademarked property
of Twentieth Century Fox Film Corporation. Used with permission. All rights reserved.

ISBN 0-590-51299-4

Copyright © 1993 by Matt Groening Productions, Inc. All rights reserved. Published by Scholastic Inc.,
555 Broadway, New York, NY 10012, by arrangement with HarperCollins Publishers. SCHOLASTIC and
associated logos are trademarks and/or registered trademarks of Scholastic Inc.

12 11 10 9 8 7   2 3/0

Printed in the U.S.A.   08

First Scholastic printing, September 1998

Concepts, Design, and Art Direction: Cindy Vance and Steve Vance
Artist: Bill Morrison
Editor: Wendy Wolf
Legal advisor: Susan Grode

Have you given a cartoonist a backrub today?

THE WEIRD WORLD OF CARTOONING, SIMPSONS-STYLE

IT SEEMS LIKE ONLY YESTERDAY THAT I WAS TEN YEARS OLD, MAN, SITTING AT MY DESK IN THE BACK OF THE CLASS, DOODLING AWAY, WHEN ALL OF A SUDDEN MY TEACHER SNUCK UP, GAVE MY KNUCKLES A GOOD RAP WITH A STEEL RULER, SNATCHED UP MY DOODLES, RIPPED THEM INTO LITTLE PIECES, DROPPED THE CONFETTI IN THE WASTEPAPER BASKET, AND LECTURED ME ABOUT NOT DRAWING STUPID LITTLE CARTOONS WHEN I SHOULD BE PAYING ATTENTION TO THE FILMSTRIP ABOUT HOW BEAVERS BUILD THEIR DAMS, YOUNG MAN!

REVENGE AGAINST INSENSITIVE GROWN-UPS IS THE STANDARD EXPLANATION THAT MOST WISE-GUY CARTOONISTS GIVE FOR WHY THEY DO WHAT THEY DO. THAT APPLIES TO ME, TOO. BUT WHAT IS SO WEIRD IN MY CASE IS THIS -- HERE COMES THE TRUE DEEP-DOWN SECRET CONFESSION:

I DON'T EXACTLY DRAW SO GOOD.

IN FACT, MOST OF MY FRIENDS BACK THEN COULD DRAW BETTER THAN I COULD. THEIR PICTURES ACTUALLY LOOKED LIKE WHAT THEY WERE SUPPOSED TO BE -- CARS AND PLANES AND GUNS AND SUPERHEROES AND NAKED LADIES -- WHILE I BASICALLY DREW CRUDE AND FUNKY BART SIMPSON-TYPE CHARACTERS OVER AND OVER AGAIN. I KNEW MY STUFF DIDN'T LOOK TOO HOT, BUT I KEPT IT UP, NO MATTER HOW CRUMMY THE DRAWING WAS. MY MORE TALENTED FRIENDS GREW UP, GOT MATURE, AND PUT ASIDE CARTOONING FOR MORE SERIOUS PURSUITS. THEY'RE NOW BORING OLD DOCTORS AND LAWYERS AND BUSINESS EXECS. I, ON THE OTHER HAND, WENT ON TO HIT THE DOODLERS' JACKPOT.

WHICH JUST GOES TO SHOW YOU.

BEFORE THE RULES: MY FIRST DRAWING OF THE SIMPSONS.

SO HERE'S MY ADVICE:

1) KEEP THINGS SIMPLE. YOU CAN CONVEY SPACE, MOTION, AND FEELING WITH SURPRISINGLY FEW LINES. LOTS OF CARTOONISTS WHO SHOULD KNOW BETTER ADD COMPLICATED DETAILS TO THEIR DRAWINGS THAT MERELY CLUTTER THINGS UP.

2) DON'T JUST FOLLOW THE "RULES" FOR DRAWING THE SIMPSONS IN THIS BOOK. THE RULES WERE INVENTED SO A LOT OF PROFESSIONAL ARTISTS, DESIGNERS, AND ANIMATORS COULD MAKE THE CHARACTERS LOOK THE SAME WAY EVERY TIME. BUT I'VE RARELY FOLLOWED THOSE RULES MYSELF. I DRAW BY INSTINCT, AND THAT'S HOW I ORIGINALLY DESIGNED THE CHARACTERS -- WITHOUT ANY RULES IN MIND.

3) DON'T BE AFRAID TO MAKE BAD DRAWINGS. STAY LOOSE AND TAKE CHANCES. EVEN DRAWINGS THAT AREN'T GREAT MIGHT HAVE GREAT DETAILS. SOMETIMES AN ACCIDENT OR A MISTAKE LEADS TO A DISCOVERY. I OFTEN FORCE MYSELF TO DRAW "THE WRONG WAY," JUST TO SEE IF I CAN COME UP WITH SOMETHING ORIGINAL.

4) SAVE YOUR STUFF! ALL OF IT, EVEN THOUGH YOUR MOM THREATENS YOUR LIFE. I GUARANTEE YOU'LL GET A KICK OUT OF YOUR OLD DRAWINGS LATER, NO MATTER WHAT YOU THINK OF THEM RIGHT NOW.

5) DON'T JUST COPY THE SIMPSONS. TRY INVENTING YOUR OWN CARTOONS. I USED TO DRAW MICKEY MOUSE, POPEYE, BATMAN, AND CHARLIE BROWN WHEN I WAS A KID. I LEARNED A LOT ABOUT DRAWING THAT WAY, BUT I SURE NEVER LEARNED HOW TO DRAW THOSE CHARACTERS CORRECTLY. IT WASN'T UNTIL I REALIZED I'D NEVER BE ABLE TO DRAW "RIGHT" THAT I ALLOWED MYSELF TO CREATE MY OWN DRAWING STYLE -- CHARACTERS WITH ULTRA-BULGY EYEBALLS AND FREAKISH OVERBITES.

FOR ME, THAT'S WHEN THE FUN BEGAN.

KEEP ON CARTOONING!

MATT GROENING

THE TECHNICAL STUFF

When I was a kid, looking at comics and magazines was both inspiring and discouraging. It was great to see the clean, perfect drawings by professional cartoonists, but it made my own stuff look messy and crude by comparison. The pros never seemed to smudge their work or put a line in the wrong place or even change their minds about what they wanted to draw.

Finally, I learned the secret: the pros <u>do</u> make mistakes -- they just know how to fix them. The drawings I was seeing in print were the result of a process of refinement. Most cartoonists start out doing pencil sketches that are almost as messy as my drawings. They sketch -- starting with very simple shapes -- until they have a composition they're happy with. Then they do a tighter pencil drawing based on the sketch. Finally, they draw over the pencil drawing in ink and erase all the pencil lines, leaving a clean finished drawing.

For sketches, I use a #2 pencil and any scrap of paper I have lying around. I'm reluctant to use most felt-tip pens, because the ink fades away after a few years (and even faster when left exposed to the sunlight).

When I'm making drawings for publication (such as my weekly comic strip "Life In Hell"), I start out with rough pencil drawings on large graph paper. (I work about 50% larger than the final printed size -- reducing the drawings helps the shaky lines look less shaky.) I use a Staedtler Mars plastic eraser, which doesn't tear up the paper the way the pink one on your pencil does. Then I put the sketch on a light box (a glass-topped box with light bulbs inside -- back before I had one of these, I'd hold the paper up against a window) and trace the whole thing onto acid-free 2-ply bristol board paper (available at most art supply stores). I use a variety of Rapidograph pens of varying sizes to get lines of different thicknesses. Rapidographs are expensive and clog easily, but they seem to encourage careful drawing, and they make your work look slick and professional. When I do make a mistake in inking, I cover it up with white opaquing paint. (If I'm desperate, I use Liquid Paper.)

In this book, we demonstrate the whole process, starting with sketching the basic shapes and working up to the finished inked drawings. To make the book more fun to look at, we've added color to some of the black and white drawings using a computer. Believe it or not, this is how most comic books and Sunday newspaper cartoons are now colored, but watercolors, crayons, colored pencils, or felt-tip pens will do the job, too.

Lots of cartoonists use other stuff, such as brushes and crow quill pens. I'm too clumsy to control these kinds of tools, but you might want to experiment to see if you can handle them.

BART

CANNED EYES

BART'S BASIC HEAD SHAPE IS A CYLINDER, KINDA LIKE A TIN CAN.

CURVED

THERE'S A VERY SLIGHT FLARE AT THE TOP OF BART'S HEAD.

THE EYE AND NOSE LINE UP, MAN.

BART HAS NINE POINTS OF HAIR:

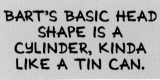

TOO PUFFY

TOO SHARP

A-OHH-KAY!

— SOFT CORNER

CURVED

LISA

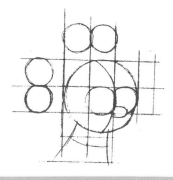  

LISA HAS 8 POINTS OF HAIR, WHICH ARE CONSTRUCTED IN GROUPS OF 3 - 3 - 2

3

3

2

WATCH THEM LASHES!

NO!!

YEAH!!

HER NECKLACE IS OFF-CENTER ON HER NECK.

MAGGIE

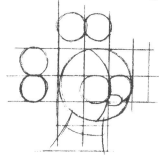  

MAGGIE'S HAIR IS A LOT LIKE LISA'S, BUT STUBBIER. IT HAS 8 POINTS THAT ARE CONSTRUCTED IN GROUPS OF 3 - 3 - 2.

3

3

3

2

MAGGIE'S EYELASHES ARE LIKE LISA'S, BUT SHE HAS ONLY THREE OF 'EM:

NO!

YES!!

MARGE

MARGE'S HAIR IS HIDING TWO BOWLING BALLS.

SAME LASHES AS LISA AND MAGGIE.

NO!

YES!!

HOMER

THINK OF HOMER'S HAIR AS TWO CROQUET HOOPS!

HOMER'S NOSE CURVES UP JUST A BIT:

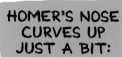

NOTE HOW THE "M" RESTS ON HOMER'S HEAD

THE MOUTH IS CONSTRUCTED LIKE TWO COCONUT HALVES:

THE COLLAR SITS A TRIFLE BELOW THE CHIN LINE

THE EYEBALL CONNECTION:

THE HEIGHT OF EACH OF THE SIMPSONS' HEADS IS EASILY MEASURED BY USING THE EYEBALL TEST.

HOMER IS SIX EYES TALL, WHILE MARGE IS NINE.

BART AND LISA ARE EACH FIVE EYES TALL. MAGGIE IS FOUR-AND-A-HALF.

THE EYES OF SIMPSONS ARE UPON YOU

HERE'S HOW THE SIMPSONS BLINK: THE TOP AND BOTTOM EYELIDS MEET IN THE MIDDLE, RATHER THAN THE TOP ONE COMING DOWN.

1

2

3

4

SIDE VIEW OF THE BLINK

FROM THE FRONT, THE NOSE OVERLAPS THE EYES.

THE FEMALE SIMPSONS HAVE EYELASHES. BE SURE THAT THEY CURL!

YES!

NO!

LIKE THIS. . .

. . . NOT THIS!

NO!

NO!!

YES!

THE EYES DON'T SIT IN FRONT OF THE NOSE, BUT THEY AREN'T HIDDEN BY THE NOSE EITHER.

DON'T CROSS THE EYES!!

NO!

YEAH!

DON'T USE A COMPLETE CIRCLE FOR THE EYELID.

EXPRESSING EMOTIONS

ALTERING JUST A FEW LINES CAN CHANGE A CHARACTER'S EMOTIONS COMPLETELY -- FROM HAPPY TO MAD, FROM BORED TO HYSTERICAL.

WORRIED

STARTLED

DOUBTFUL

CONTENTED

FRIGHTENED

EXCITED

SURPRISED

LOVEY-DOVEY

EMBARRASSED

HAGGARD

FUMING

AGITATED

HORRIFIED

PEEVISH

APPALLED

MELANCHOLY

BLUE

ASTONISHED

MIRTHFUL

DREAMY

SARCASTIC

GIGGLY

STUNNED

BORED

SHOCKED

HYSTERICAL

AWED

WOOZY

DISTRESSED

CHEERY

ANGST-RIDDEN

SELF-DISGUSTED

DELIGHTED

TERRIFIED

INFURIATED

FEARFUL

GUILTY

STUFFED

DEJECTED

NORMAL

MOVIN' 'N' GROOVIN'

THE SIMPSONS MOVE AND BEND LIKE REAL PEOPLE!

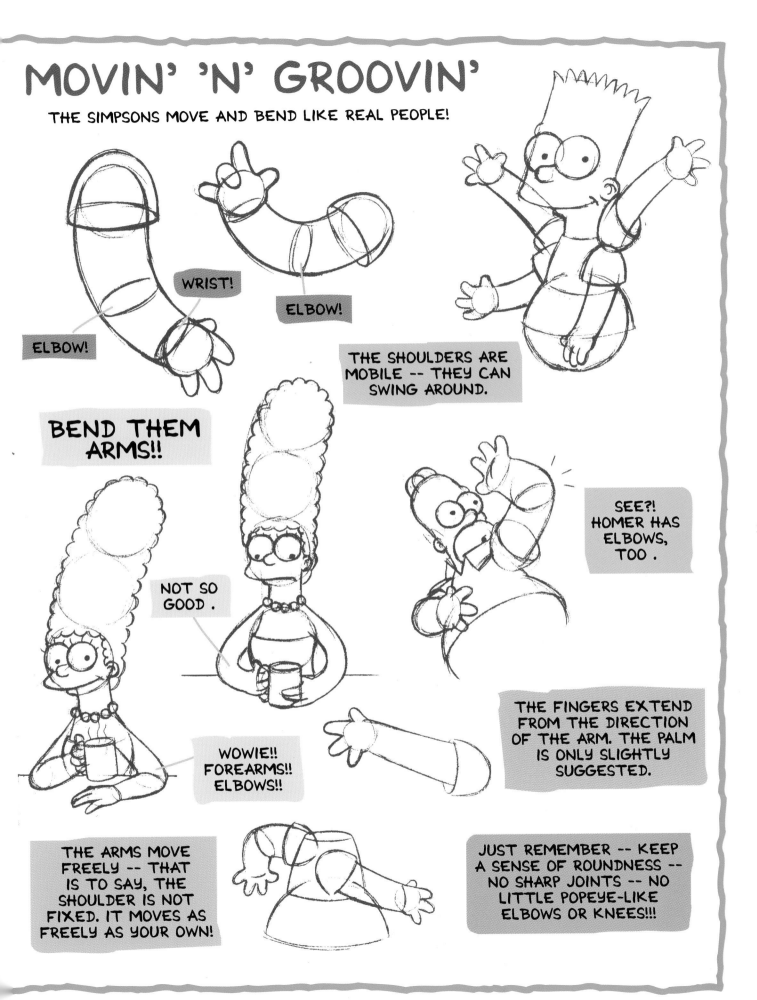

WRIST!

ELBOW!

ELBOW!

THE SHOULDERS ARE MOBILE -- THEY CAN SWING AROUND.

BEND THEM ARMS!!

NOT SO GOOD .

SEE?! HOMER HAS ELBOWS, TOO .

WOWIE!! FOREARMS!! ELBOWS!!

THE FINGERS EXTEND FROM THE DIRECTION OF THE ARM. THE PALM IS ONLY SLIGHTLY SUGGESTED.

THE ARMS MOVE FREELY -- THAT IS TO SAY, THE SHOULDER IS NOT FIXED. IT MOVES AS FREELY AS YOUR OWN!

JUST REMEMBER -- KEEP A SENSE OF ROUNDNESS -- NO SHARP JOINTS -- NO LITTLE POPEYE-LIKE ELBOWS OR KNEES!!!

MAGGIE'S HANDS

BART AND LISA'S HANDS

LISA'S FEET

BART'S FEET

THE CIRCULAR LABELS ARE ONLY ON THE INSIDES OF BART'S SHOES.

MARGE'S HANDS AND FEET

HOMER'S HANDS AND FEET

LIGHTS! PENCILS! ACTION!

YOU'VE STUDIED THE BASICS -- NOW SEE HOW ALL THE PIECES FIT TOGETHER.

When David Silverman was first hired to help animate the Simpsons, he assumed the job would last three weeks. Six years later, he is a supervising director for the series. Wes Archer, one of the other original Simpsons animators, has directed many episodes. The two of them are largely responsible for the show's look and the way the characters move. Together, they helped develop the bible on how to draw the Simpsons, and a lot of the ideas in this book come from their notes.

Thanks go to Cindy and Steve Vance, who conceived and created this book, and to Bill Morrison, who did most of the actual drawings. And special thanks to everyone who has ever rendered the Simpsons professionally: cartoonists, graphic designers, costume makers, video game programmers, toy figurine sculptors, giant parade-balloon inflators, and - - oh yes - - animators.